# A.I. FOR ANYBODY

*The Non-Coder's Guide to*
*Understanding Artificial Intelligence*

## NICHOLAS PELLEGRINO

ISBN: 9798637826872

Published by Game Quill LLC.

Created & Printed in the United States of America.

First Edition.

www.GameQuill.com

*For my parents, Louis Pellegrino & Joan Pellegrino, who always supported me*

# TABLE OF CONTENTS

# Introduction

Artificial intelligence is a mysterious subject to the public eye because computer scientists often find it too complicated to explain. My goal with this book is to take some of the complex mathematical concepts that make A.I. work and make them super simple for anyone to understand.

Too often we read news and watch movies with a common theme: robots and artificial intelligence could be a danger to the human race. But what is artificial intelligence? How does it work? Is it sentient? Will it ever be? Should you be afraid of it? It's hard to form a solid opinion about artificial intelligence if you don't even understand how it works.

A.I. is an advanced computer science topic. It is rarely explained well to the general public. Most "Understanding Artificial Intelligence" books are aimed at coders and mathematicians who are coming in with an advanced skill set already. This book only assumes you know how to multiply two numbers together.

I will simplify this advanced topic into easy-to-understand segments, perfect for even a non-coder. Chapters 1-3 will have clear explanations and diagrams that teach you what artificial intelligence is and how a computer "learns" things. Chapter 3 will even go as far as to apply this new knowledge to build a simple machine learning A.I. and show you how it works under the hood. Chapters 4-7 will then expand this example to reveal how that same A.I. system can be implemented in many totally different situations. Chapter 8 is where we end our journey by finally discussing the actual dangers of A.I. - a conversation that will be much easier to have when you understand how A.I. works.

See you on the other side,

*- Nick Pellegrino*

# A.I. FOR ANYBODY

# Chapter 1: What is Artificial Intelligence?

For those of you in a hurry, I'll answer the question immediately: artificial intelligence is purely MATHEMATICS. That's the answer. Artificial intelligence is NOT SENTIENT - it is a mathematical formula that does stuff.

What stuff does it do? Anything! You just have to be clever about how you create the math formula.

So how do you create the math formula? Simple: you use a man-made math formula to analyze a bunch of data and output this new magical math formula. This is the "learning" that a computer goes through. Chapter 3 will go into more detail about that. But before we go deep into detail, let's talk about artificial intelligence in general.

~ ~ ~

## History of Artificial Intelligence

The definition of "artificial intelligence" has changed over the years. In the past, before the days of powerful computers, the term was simply used to describe a computer acting intelligently.

Think of games like "Pong" by Atari, for example. Pong is a game where the player has two inputs: "up" and "down." In this game, the player controls a paddle and can move it up and down in an attempt to block the ball from going into their goal. At the same time, another player controls a paddle and is trying to do the same thing. You win a point when the opponent fails to block the ball before you do.

Artist's Rendering. Not an actual screenshot of Pong.

In most cases, another human is playing the second paddle; but as time went on, some coders eventually designed an "artificial intelligence" for single players to play against. This "Pong A.I." was simply a math function that told the paddle to go "up" when the ball was higher than the paddle and "down" when the ball was lower. This created a seemingly intelligent program that looked like it was trying to hit the ball when in reality it was just following some simple instructions.

These days, "artificial intelligence" means far more. One type of artificial intelligence, called "machine learning," involves code that "learns" based on data. For example, a machine learning version of the Pong A.I. would look at data from people playing Pong and subsequently learn complex behaviors instead of just following the ball based on two simple rules.

These complex behaviors, however, are *still* just the program following instructions. The instructions are insanely complicated, but easy for a computer to follow. This artificial intelligence program is much "smarter" than the old versions of A.I., but it still is just following instructions. The difference is that a human didn't write the instructions – an algorithm for machine learning did, but neither that algorithm nor the new machine learning Pong A.I. is sentient.

*The artificial intelligence program is still just following instructions. The difference is that a human didn't write the instructions - an algorithm for machine learning did.*

~ ~ ~

## The Neural Network

There are many types of learning artificial intelligence out there. I could talk for hours and hours about a number of them, but that wouldn't accomplish the goal of this book: to teach a non-coder how A.I. works. To prevent confusion, we will only talk about one type of artificial intelligence in this book.

I have chosen to teach you about the type of A.I. known as a "neural network." The neural network is a type of artificial intelligence fundamental to the machine learning field.

Why the neural network? I chose neural networks because they are the type of A.I. you will most often encounter. When you read articles with buzzwords like "deep learning," "machine learning," "hidden layers," and, well, "artificial intelligence," more often than not they are talking about some form of a neural network.

Neural networks are also such an integrated part of this field that I'm betting they won't be going anywhere anytime soon. They will advance, but the general idea of a neural network will stay. This ensures that what I'm about to teach you will not quickly become outdated.

The artificial intelligence profession is expanding at an incredible rate. The field looks entirely different now than it did five years ago - and it'll change again in the next five years. Even the average computer scientist often struggles to keep up with this rapidly evolving discipline. Neural networks, however, are part of the foundation of the field. While more advanced forms of neural networks are being made all the time, the generic neural network hasn't become obsolete, and probably won't be for many years.

~ ~ ~

## Conclusion

The basic idea behind neural networks is this: you store data in something called a matrix, you give that matrix to your neural network, and then your neural network performs an algorithm called matrix multiplication on that data in a special way so that it can output an answer to whatever question you're asking it.

So, what do all those words mean? What is a matrix? What is matrix multiplication? Those questions and more are answered by a branch of mathematics called "linear algebra."

~ ~ ~

# Chapter 2: What is Linear Algebra?

Just like geometry, calculus, and statistics, linear algebra is a branch of mathematics. Linear algebra is quite important for machine learning algorithms. Neural networks, for example, need a linear algebra function called "matrix multiplication" in order to work.

If we're going to go into detail about neural networks in chapter 3, we first must discuss matrix multiplication, as well as the concept of a "matrix" in general, here in chapter 2.

The matrix, or "matrices" for plural, is a structure used by computers for storing data. Computers store all sorts of data in matrices. Consider, for example, this photograph of my dog:

This image is stored on my computer using a matrix. So, what does that mean? What is a matrix?

To start, let's take a few steps back. Let's first talk about how computers store numbers, and then build our way up to images & matrices!

~ ~ ~

### The Data Point

To start, let's just store a single number in our computer's memory. To do so, we write a line of code:

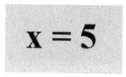

Alright, so what did that do? Well, we created a spot in our computer's memory that can hold a number. Let's call this a "data point." We arbitrarily named our data point "x" and we gave it a value of 5.

So, what did the computer do with that instruction? Let's look under the hood, at the computer's memory:

Our data point looks like a little gray block labeled "x." Since it's just a data point, it's quite small - only big enough to hold a single number. It appears to be holding the number 5.

Let's write some more code:

$$x = 5$$
$$y = 3$$
$$z = x \cdot y$$

This code created three data points in our computer's memory. We've arbitrarily named them x, y, and z. We put 5 into x, 3 into y, and told z to hold the product of x times y. Let's see what happened:

Alright! Our computer's memory has some new stuff. We have a data point named "x" holding 5, a data point named "y" holding 3, and a data point named "z" holding 15 (because 5 x 3 = 15). In total, we have three data points in our computer's memory.

~ ~ ~

## The Array

Now we're going to take a step upwards in our dimensions. Instead of storing just one number into a data point, we are going to store *multiple* numbers into something called an "array." An "array" in computer science is similar to a "set" in mathematics. You can think of it as a collection of data points forming a straight line.

Let's make an array:

$$a = [1, 1, 3, 5]$$

That line of code created an array of four numbers. Let's check out how the computer stored it:

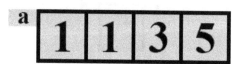

There it is! We have an array of numbers and we named it "a." The data in our array is called the array's "elements." In this example, our array has four elements. The first element is 1, the second element is also 1, the third element is 3, and the fourth element is 5. Instead of having four different data points with different names, we can access all four of our numbers just by looking at our one array.

Let's make some more arrays:

$$a = [1, 1, 3, 5]$$
$$b = [5, 0, 5, 0]$$
$$c = [2, 4, 6, 8]$$

And let's see what the computer did with that:

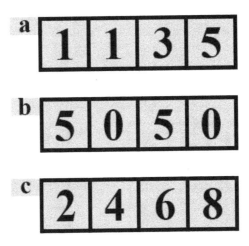

Great! We have three arrays.

~ ~ ~

## The Matrix

I have a weird idea. What if we take our three arrays and put them together *into another array?* I'm talking about an array *of arrays*.

Let's give it a try:

$$a = [1, 1, 3, 5]$$
$$b = [5, 0, 5, 0]$$
$$c = [2, 4, 6, 8]$$
$$m = [a, b, c]$$

In this code, we first make our three arrays a, b, and c again just like last time. We then make m to be an array *of arrays a, b, and c!*

What do you think will happen? Let's check it out:

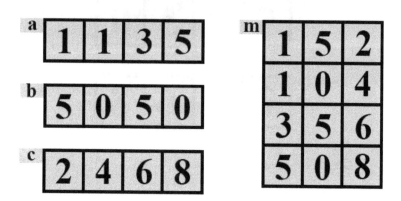

Alright! We created an *array of arrays* named "m." Instead of a line of data, we now have a *rectangle* of data! **This is a matrix!**

We now have our definition. **A matrix is a rectangle of data.** So what? Why did someone bother making a branch of mathematics that does calculations with these things?

You're not alone in having that question. Professional mathematicians have told me that they never understood the purpose of learning linear algebra in college - but that's because they're not working with computers. We are. And computers use this concept to store *all sorts of data.* For example, your computer views black-and-white images as a matrix.

~ ~ ~

## The Image as a Matrix

When your computer has to store a black-and-white image, it stores it as a matrix of numbers ranging from 0 to 255, where 0 represents a black pixel, 255 represents a white pixel, and anything in between is a shade of gray:

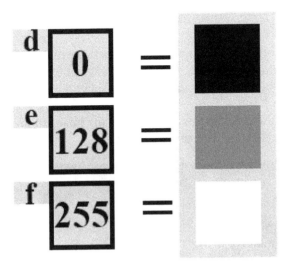

In this example, the three data points d, e, and f are acting like matrices of size 1 x 1. Each 1 x 1 matrix holds a single pixel value. The matrix d is holding a single 0, so it has one black pixel. The matrix f is holding 255, so it has a white pixel. The matrix e is holding 128, so it has a shade of gray in between black and white.

Instead of boring 1 x 1 matrices, let's look at a more substantial matrix. Here is a 3 x 4 matrix named "m." It contains pixel color values. On the right side, you can see what "m" looks like as an image:

m

| 0 | 50 | 100 | 150 |
|---|----|-----|-----|
| 200 | 250 | 255 | 0 |
| 0 | 87 | 23 | 192 |

=

Notice how numbers closer to 0 are darker shades while numbers closer to 255 are lighter. This range of 0 to 255 covers every shade of gray that your computer can display.

Now consider this black-and-white image of my dog (he is a Goldendoodle and his name is Linus):

You see a black-and-white image here, but the computer sees a matrix. The matrix is size 730 x 556, and it's full of numbers ranging between 0 and 255. Each of those numbers represents a pixel in our image, and the value of the number describes the color.

It would take up a lot of the page to show you a matrix of size 730 x 556, so let's zoom in a little bit. Here's a 28 x 47 close-up of his eyes:

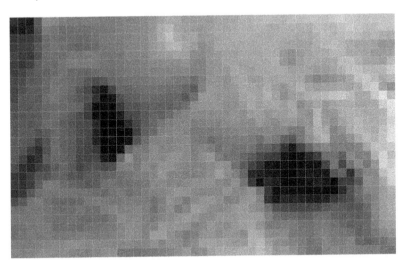

Now that we've zoomed in, it's easier to see that the image is made up of pixels. Let's take a look at the matrix for this image:

You can see that the areas of the image which are darker, such as the center of his eyes, are small, single-digit or double-digit values, whereas the areas of the image that are lighter, like his fur, have triple-digit values.

Here they are next to each other:

Image You See (28 x 47 pixels)      Matrix the Computer Uses (28 x 47 numbers)

A matrix can be used for more than just images, but we'll worry about that in later chapters.

~ ~ ~

## Matrix Multiplication

For the final concept in this chapter, we're going to look at a linear algebra method called *matrix multiplication*, which is the idea of multiplying two matrices together.

Matrix multiplication is a process that involves combining two matrices. This is done by combining each row of one matrix with each column of a second matrix.

Before we start combining any numbers together, we need to think about the rectangle shape of our matrices. In order to have each row in the first matrix combine with each column in the second matrix, we need to cancel out the number of columns in the first with the number of rows in the second matrix.

The rectangle shape of a matrix can be described as rows x columns, or height x width. You've already seen me describe matrices this way - I described the zoomed-in picture of my dog's eyes as a 28 x 47 matrix because its height is 28 and its width is 47. That is to say, the image was 28 rows of pixels by 47 columns of pixels.

If I were to multiply that 28 x 47 matrix with another matrix, the second matrix would HAVE to have a height of 47. This is because we need 47 rows of pixels in the second image to cancel out the 47 columns of pixels in our image of my dog's eyes.

I could multiply our 28 x 47 matrix with a 47 x 8 matrix, for example, because the 47 x 8 matrix has a height of 47. This means our first matrix's 47 columns have 47 rows from the second matrix to cancel out with.

I would not be able to multiply our 28 x 47 matrix with an 8 x 47 matrix because that matrix has a height of 8, not 47. The 47 rows would line up with 8 columns, and that's unequal, so the rectangle shapes wouldn't cancel out together.

Another way to look at this is that the middle numbers need to "match up." For example, in a multiplication of 28 x 47 with 47 x 8, the 47's match up. When we try to multiply 28 x 47 with 8 x 47, the 47 and 8 match up, which is invalid.

This might be getting confusing, so let's look at an example with smaller matrices. For simplicity's sake, I'm not going to fill the matrices with numbers quite yet:

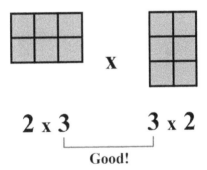

$$2 \times 3 \qquad 3 \times 2$$

**Good!**

Multiplying a 2 x 3 matrix with a 3 x 2 matrix is a valid calculation because the 3's match up. Do you think it would be okay to multiply a 2 x 3 matrix with a 3 x 3 matrix? Let's find out:

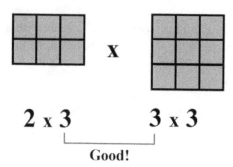

**Good!**

It is okay! Multiplying a 2 x 3 matrix with a 3 x 3 matrix is also a valid calculation for the same reason: the 3's match. Next question: how about a 2 x 3 matrix with another 2 x 3 matrix? Let's find out:

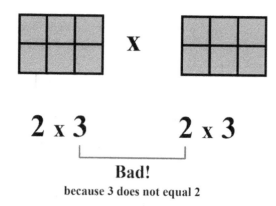

**Bad!**

because 3 does not equal 2

Multiplying a 2 x 3 matrix with a 2 x 3 matrix is NOT a valid calculation because the 3 isn't paired with another 3 - it's paired with a 2!

Hopefully, you've caught the pattern at this point: the height of the first matrix and the width of the second matrix can be anything, but the width of the first matrix and the height of the second matrix must be equal.

The next thing you need to know about rectangle shapes is this: the solution for our equation is a matrix with a rectangle shape equal to the height of the first matrix x the width of the second matrix. Check it out:

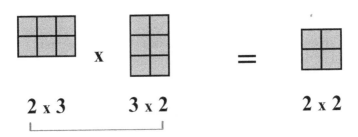

That's our example where we multiply a 2 x 3 matrix with a 3 x 2 matrix. We know this is a valid calculation because the 3's match - but now, we can also see why that's important: the 3's cancel each other out, and we are left with a 2 x 2 matrix as our solution.

This is because matrix multiplication is all about combining that first matrix's rows with the second matrix's columns. Our 2 x 3 matrix has 2 rows, and our 3 x 2 matrix has 2 columns. When we combine 2 rows with 2 columns, we get a 2 x 2 matrix as our solution.

So, how do we combine 2 rows with 2 columns? Let's solve a real equation so we can see how it happens. To start, I'll fill in our matrices with some numbers and show you the final solution:

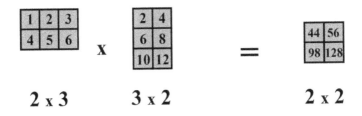

In this example, we perform matrix multiplication on a 2 x 3

matrix with a 3 x 2 matrix. The 3's match up, and thus cancel out, leaving us with a 2 x 2 matrix solution.

Our solution is 2 x 2 because we are combining 2 rows (from the first matrix) with 2 columns (from the second matrix). There are exactly 2 x 2 ways to combine 2 rows with 2 columns.

How do we combine a row with a column? We multiply each element of the row with its respective element in the column and then add everything together.

For example, let's combine row 1 with column 1. Row 1 in our example is [1, 2, 3]. That means 1 is the first element of the row, 2 is the second, and 3 is the third. Column 1 in our example is [2, 6, 10]. That means 2 is the first element of the column, 6 is the second, and 10 is the third.

To combine [1, 2, 3] with [2, 6, 10], we first multiply each element with its pair. The first elements go together: (1 x 2 = 2), the second elements go together: (2 x 6 = 12), and the third elements go together: (3 x 10 = 30). We then just add those solutions together: (2 + 12 + 30 = 44).

This 44 represents row 1 combined with column 1, so it goes in the (row 1, col 1) space in our final matrix. That's the top-left slot of our 2 x 2 solution matrix!

Here's everything we just did, but shown visually:

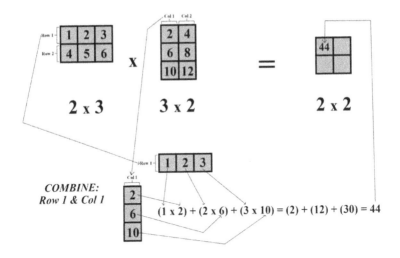

COMBINE:
Row 1 & Col 1

$(1 \times 2) + (2 \times 6) + (3 \times 10) = (2) + (12) + (30) = 44$

We combined row 1 and column 1 to get 44.

The next spot we want to fill in our 2 x 2 solution matrix is the top-right slot, or the (row 1, col 2) slot. To do so, we combine row 1 of the first matrix with col 2 of the second matrix:

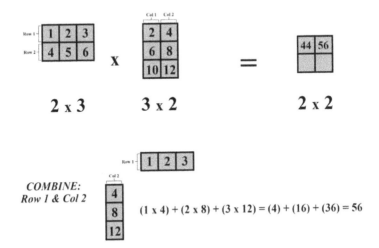

COMBINE:
Row 1 & Col 2

$(1 \times 4) + (2 \times 8) + (3 \times 12) = (4) + (16) + (36) = 56$

Just like with 44, this is done by multiplying each of the three elements with their pair, then adding all those solutions together. We end up with 56 as out solution, which goes in the top-right of our 2 x 2 solution matrix.

Now, we continue the process again. We want to fill in the bottom-left of our 2 x 2 solution matrix, which is the (row 2, col 1) slot. Let's combine row 2 with column 1:

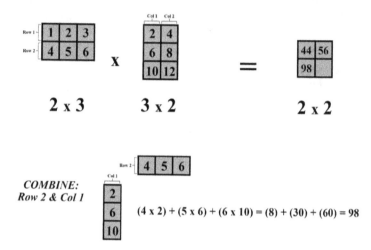

COMBINE:
Row 2 & Col 1

$(4 \times 2) + (5 \times 6) + (6 \times 10) = (8) + (30) + (60) = 98$

We combined row 2 with column 1 and found that the answer was 98. We put that 98 in our 2 x 2 solution matrix.

Now there's just one more combination we haven't tried yet: row 2 with column 2. Let's do it:

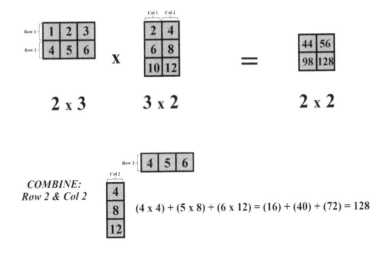

As you can see, we combine column 2 with row 2 and get a solution of 128.

Our 2 x 2 solution matrix is now full. We've successfully performed matrix multiplication!

*~ ~ ~ Fun Fact: ~ ~ ~*

*This process of combining rows and columns, where we multiply each element with its pair and then add all the answers together, is called a **dot product**. The solution matrix for a matrix multiplication problem can be described as "a matrix which holds the dot product for every row in the first matrix with every column in the second matrix"*

~ ~ ~ ~ ~ ~ ~ ~ ~ ~

Let's look at another example:

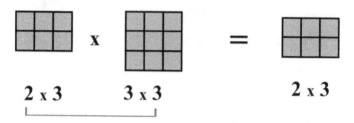

**2 x 3**　　　**3 x 3**　　　　　　**2 x 3**

We've got an empty 2 x 3 matrix being multiplied by an empty 3 x 3 matrix. The 3's cancel out and leave us with a 2 x 3 matrix as our output.

To fill in the 2 x 3 solution matrix, we would do 6 calculations: every possible combination of 2 rows with 3 columns.

Let's add some arbitrary numbers to our first two matrices and take a look at the solution:

| 2 | 4 | 6 |
|---|---|---|
| 0 | 1 | 0 |

X

| 1 | 2 | 3 |
|---|---|---|
| 4 | 5 | 6 |
| 5 | 0 | 5 |

=

| 48 | 24 | 60 |
|----|----|----|
| 4 | 5 | 6 |

Here are the 6 equations we would need to solve to fill in that 2 x 3 solution matrix:

$$(2 \times 1) + (4 \times 4) + (6 \times 5) = (2) + (16) + (30) = 48$$
$$(2 \times 2) + (4 \times 5) + (6 \times 0) = (4) + (20) + (0) = 24$$
$$(2 \times 3) + (4 \times 6) + (6 \times 5) = (6) + (24) + (30) = 60$$
$$(0 \times 1) + (1 \times 4) + (0 \times 5) = (0) + (4) + (0) = 4$$
$$(0 \times 2) + (1 \times 5) + (0 \times 0) = (0) + (5) + (0) = 5$$
$$(0 \times 3) + (1 \times 6) + (0 \times 5) = (0) + (6) + (0) = 6$$

~ ~ ~

## Applying What We've Learned

When it comes to neural networks, we're more concerned about manipulating the shapes of matrices than the actual process of calculating matrix multiplication, since the actual mathematical calculations can just be done by some computer code.

What we're after is using matrix multiplication as a tool to change the size of our matrix. For example, let's say I have a 2 x 3 matrix, but I want a 2 x 2 matrix.

You know that this can be achieved if you provide me with a 3 x 2 matrix, since the 3's will cancel out and leave us with a 2 x 2 solution:

| 1 | 2 | 3 |
|---|---|---|
| 4 | 5 | 6 |

X

| 2 | 4 |
|---|---|
| 6 | 8 |
| 10 | 12 |

=

| 44 | 56 |
|----|----|
| 98 | 128 |

**2 x 3**         **3 x 2**                    **2 x 2**

Alternatively, let's say I want a 2 x 5 solution matrix. Then, you can set up my matrix multiplication by providing a 3 x 5 matrix.

That would allow me to perform matrix multiplication to turn a 2 x 3 image into a 2 x 5 solution matrix, since 2 x 3 with 3 x 5 = 2 x 5.

*If you're careful about your rectangle shapes, you have a lot of power over what your solution looks like!*

Let's say I next give you a picture of my dog's eyes, which we know is a 28 x 47 matrix, and I tell you that I want you to convert it into a 28 x 10 matrix.

You now know that this can be achieved by supplying a 47 x 10 matrix since 28 x 47 with 47 x 10 cancels out the 47's to create a 28 x 10 matrix!

Hmm… where could we find a 47 x 10 matrix? Well, since images are matrices, I'll just draw a little 47-pixel by 10-pixel image for us to use:

Sweet! Now we have a 47 x 10 image (matrix) to complement our 28 x 47 image (matrix) of my dog's eyes. Let's use matrix multiplication to combine these two pictures together and see what happens (Note: I normalized the output to be in the range between 0 and 255, so the result could be viewed as an image):

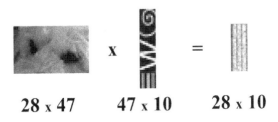

**28 x 47**     **47 x 10**     **28 x 10**

Neat! Our solution contains data from both images. It's also the shape we expected - the same height as our first image and the same width as our second image.

~ ~ ~

## Conclusion

What exactly did we just learn, and why?

Let's start with what we learned:

- A matrix is a rectangle of data

- Your computer views black-and-white images as a matrix of values ranging from 0 to 255

- Linear algebra proposes "matrix multiplication," which lets us combine data from two different matrices into one matrix

- We can't perform matrix multiplication on two matrices unless two of their sides cancel out

- When we perform matrix multiplication, the sides that don't cancel out define the rectangle shape of our solution

Okay, but who cares? Why did we just learn that? Well, that's what chapter 3 is for. In chapter 3, we're finally going to talk about neural networks (a type of artificial intelligence) - which are all about matrix multiplication!

~ ~ ~

# Chapter 3: What is a Neural Network?

Neural networks are a form of artificial intelligence. You can think of them as a mathematical function that accepts a matrix as input, does some matrix multiplication to it, and finally gives you a new matrix as the output. The unique thing about neural networks is that you can "train" them using data.

In this chapter, we are going to make a neural network, train it, and see it in action.

~ ~ ~

### Diagram of a Neural Network

If you've looked up neural networks or artificial intelligence in the past, you may have come across some mysterious diagrams with lots of boxes and lines. Let's take a look at one of those pictures right now and figure out what exactly is going on.

Here is a diagram of a neural network:

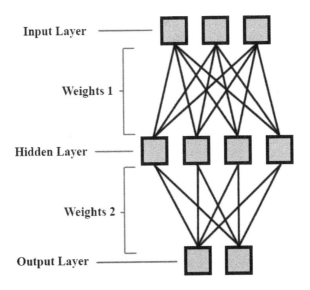

We've got a lot of buzz words going on here such as "weights" and "layers," but you might already be making some connections to chapter 2. Our "layers" here are matrices. In this particular diagram, our "Input Layer" is a 1 x 3 matrix, our "Hidden Layer" is a 1 x 4 matrix, and our "Output Layer" is a 1 x 2 matrix.

The diagram doesn't make it obvious, but our "weights" are also matrices. The "weights" are meant to be the in-between matrices that we use for matrix multiplication to move our data through the layers.

We want to perform matrix multiplication on the "Input Layer" matrix with the "Weights 1" matrix to create our "Hidden Layer" matrix.

Our "Input Layer" is a 1 x 3 matrix and our "Hidden Layer" needs to be a 1 x 4 matrix. Can you figure out the rectangle shape of "Weights 1?"

This problem is just like the one we solved at the end of chapter 2 when we wanted to turn a 28 x 47 matrix into a 28 x 10 matrix. We knew the answer was to perform matrix multiplication on our 28 x 47 matrix with a 47 x 10 matrix so the 47's cancel out, leaving behind the 28 x 10 matrix we wanted.

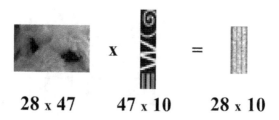

**28 x 47**　　**47 x 10**　　**28 x 10**

With this neural network, we have a 1 x 3 matrix and we want a 1 x 4 matrix. The answer is to multiply the 1 x 3 matrix by a 3 x 4 matrix. That will make the 3's cancel out and leave behind a 1 x 4 matrix, which is what we wanted for our hidden layer! Similarly, we use "Weights 2" to turn our "Hidden Layer" into our "Output Layer."

Our "Hidden Layer" is a 1 x 4 matrix, and our "Output Layer" is a 1 x 2 matrix, so "Weights 2" must be a 4 x 2 matrix. This is because when we multiply our 1 x 4 matrix by a 4 x 2 matrix, the 4's cancel out and we are left with the 1 x 2 matrix for our "Output Layer."

That was a lot of numbers to read, so here's the same diagram again, but with the matrix information we just figured out:

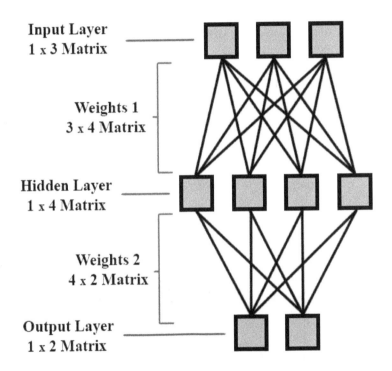

This image visually confirms our calculations for the rectangle shape of our weights. Since "Weights 1" is converting a 1 x 3 matrix into a 1 x 4 matrix, it is depicted with our 3 boxes jutting out with 4 lines each, i.e. a 3 x 4 matrix. Similarly, our 4 hidden layer boxes jut out with 2 lines each, visually confirming that "Weights 2" must be a 4 x 2 matrix.

This is happening because the math behind matrix multiplication, which we discussed in chapter 2, ensures that every piece of data in our matrices being multiplied contributes some information to the solution matrix.

~ ~ ~

## Solving Problems with a Neural Network

What's the point of all this? We have three mysterious matrices called "layers," and two matrices called "weights." Why do we want them?

The answer, my friend, is ANSWERS! This strange mathematical setup can answer *pretty much any question you could think of.* A savvy computer scientist just needs to be clever about how they design the layers. They also need some data that relates to the question.

Let's jump back to our conversation about the game Pong in chapter 1. In case you forgot, Pong is a game where the player has two inputs, "up" and "down," to control a paddle. The player tries to block a ball from going into their goal. At the same time, an opponent controls a paddle and is trying to outplay them:

Artist's Rendering. Not an actual screenshot of Pong.

Let's say we want to play Pong, but we have no friends. This is a problem for many reasons, one being that we don't have a second person available to play Pong with us. Perhaps we could build a Pong A.I. to play with us, using the neural network we've been looking at?

As I said earlier, a neural network can solve any problem if you're clever and you have some data. To start, let's assume we have some data.

The data we'll assume we have is game data from hours and hours of a human playing Pong. Every time the human player pushed "up" or "down," we collected the location of the ball on the screen (horizontal and vertical) and the location of the player's paddle (vertical location). Here's an example of a single line of data in this format:

In this line of data, we see a snapshot in time. The ball was located at an (x, y) location of (125, 50). This means the ball was 125 pixels from the left of the screen and 50 pixels down from the top of the screen. The player's paddle was 100 pixels down from the top of the screen. To make things easier, here's a picture of the situation:

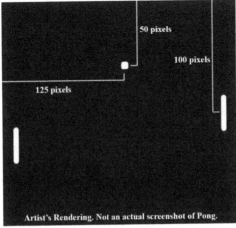

At this moment, it seems that the player was pushing "up" on the joystick. You can see this is true because the "up" data point in our data had a value of 1 and the "down" data point had a value of 0:

In computer science, we generally describe the concept of "False" as a value of 0 and the concept of "True" as any nonzero value, such as a value of 1. Therefore, we can format "yes/no" questions as a value of 1 for "yes" and a value of 0 for "no." In this case, a value of 1 for "up" means the player was pushing "up" on the joystick and not "down."

The data we just looked at represents a single moment in time. Let's say we actually had thousands, maybe even millions, of lines of data just like that. Five numbers, each showing a single moment in time across hours of gameplay. That's enough data to train a neural network!

Now that we have our data, we just need to be clever with how we set up our neural network. Conveniently, the network we've already been working with is perfect:

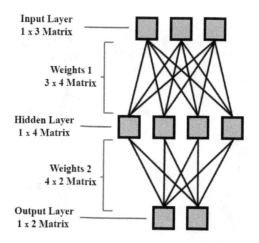

Why is this network perfect? Well, let's think about the problem we want to solve. We want to train a neural network that will play Pong. That means it has to **output** a movement, either "up" or "down." In our data, movement is represented by our "Player's Input," which consists of two data points, or a 1 x 2 matrix. You may have noticed that our "Output Layer" is a 1 x 2 matrix as well. This means our neural network will always output a 1 x 2 matrix, which we can interpret as Pong player input.

Let's make a note on our diagram that the "Output Layer" is going to represent "up" and "down" button presses:

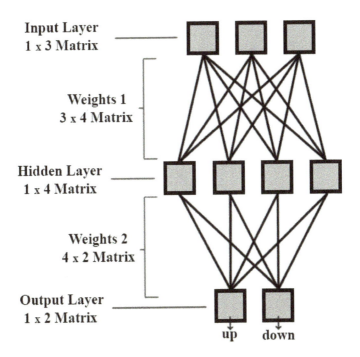

While we're talking about the output layer, let's also add an "activation function," which is just a simple math function that will normalize our output (force the values to be in a certain range). At the end of chapter 2, when we matrix multiplied two images together, you may remember that I mentioned I had "normalized" the output so each value was in the range of 0 to 255 (perfect for viewing it as an image). That's similar to what we're going to do now with an "activation function" on our output layer that forces it to be in a range useful to our situation.

Our "Player's Input" consists of 0s and 1s, so the best range for this situation is between 0 and 1. To achieve this, we will use the activation function called "softmax." The softmax activation function forces all the values in our matrix to add up to 1 based on probability. Among other things, doing this normalizes our data because it forces each number to be in a range between 0 and 1.

Here's what our Pong A.I. is looking like now:

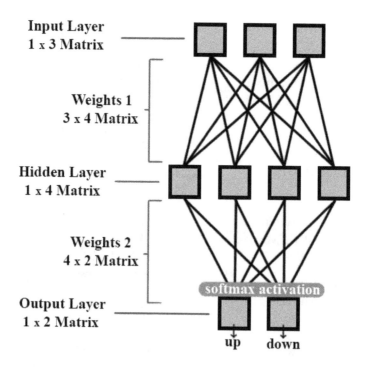

It's the same neural network we've been looking at, just with that extra boost at the end with the softmax activation function. We also still have our mental note that the neural network wants to move the paddle "up" when it outputs [1, 0] and that it wants to move the paddle "down" when it outputs [0, 1].

Although we now know how to interpret the network's output layer, we still need to give it some data so it can make a decision. This is where the input layer comes in.

Conveniently, our dataset includes 3 informational values about the locations of objects on the screen, and our input layer accepts a matrix of size 1 x 3. All we need to do is shove our 3 informational values into the input layer:

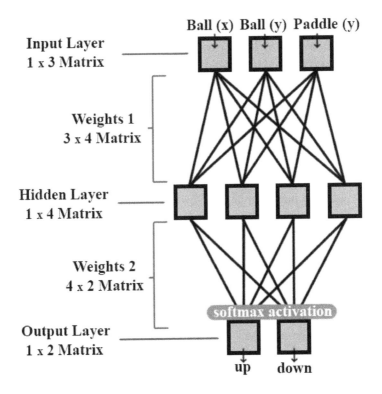

Now we have a neural network that accepts three pieces of data about Pong as input, does matrix multiplication twice, and outputs whether the paddle should go up or down. That whole process of inputting data to receive an output layer is called "feeding-forward."

The next thing we need to do is set our weights up and train the neural network.

~ ~ ~

## Weights vs. Layers

Weights and layers are both matrices. The difference is that layers are just empty placeholders waiting for data, whereas weights are matrices full of constant values. The machine's "learning" will happen when we use a mathematical formula to decide what those constant "weight" values should be.

We begin the "training/learning" process by filling our "weight" matrices with totally random values. That means "Weights 1" gets a 3 x 4 matrix of random values and "Weights 2" gets a 4 x 2 matrix of random values.

We leave our hidden layer alone - it's just a midway placeholder for our input layer as it slowly transforms into the output layer. Having this hidden layer as a midway step lets us do matrix multiplication twice - adding some complexity that will improve the accuracy of our neural network.

Alright. So, we've got some random values in our weights. What would happen if we "feed-forward" right now?

Consider a moment while playing Pong. The ball is located at an (x, y) of (50, 25). The A.I.'s paddle is located at a (y) of (40). What happens? First, our code takes the data and turns it into a 1 x 3 matrix: [50, 25, 40]. Next, it gives that data to the neural network as the input layer:

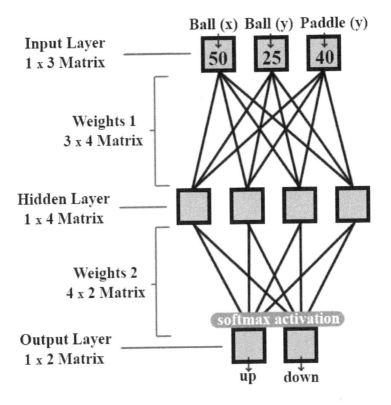

The untrained neural network receives an input layer: [50, 25, 40]. The network now does the feed-forward process to get an output layer. This means our code matrix multiplies our input layer by "Weights 1" to get the hidden layer, and then matrix multiplies that hidden layer by "Weights 2" to get the output layer. The problem is, "Weights 1" and "Weights 2" are currently full of meaningless random values.

This means the values in our output layer will just be useless nonsense. The neural network likely won't even output whole numbers. The outputs will probably be crazy things like [0.7263, 0.2737], which is useless to us. However, let's say we *trained* the neural network first. Then, we would get useful outputs from it!

~ ~ ~

## Training the Neural Network

The training process starts by creating something called a "loss function." The loss function is a mathematical algorithm that compares a neural network's feed-forward output layer with the correct answer.

Let's say we're doing a round of training with this piece of data from our dataset:

The data we've got here gives us three informational values: [50, 25, 40], as well as an "up/down" decision: [1, 0]. This means [50, 25, 40] is what we'll give to our input layer, and [1, 0] is our "correct answer" that we want the neural network to output.

Let's say we feed-forward [50, 25, 40] through our neural network and the output is [0.7263, 0.2737]. That is not the same thing as [1,0]. Our "loss function" helps our network gauge out just how incorrect that was. We can then use a mathematical process called "back propagation" to edit the "weight" matrices in a way that would minimize our "loss" value. That is to say, we edit our "weight" matrices so that the neural network would've answered closer to [1,0] when given the input layer [50, 25, 40].

~ ~ ~ *Fun Fact* ~ ~ ~

*"Loss" is a mathematical interpretation of how bad your neural network is. You can think of it as a summation of all the errors your network made. The less errors it makes, the lower the loss. The lower the loss, the better the neural network (for the most part).*

*We want to edit our "weight" matrices in a way that minimizes this "loss" value. We can achieve this by using a process called "gradient descent." Gradient descent figures out the best way to go about editing our "weight" values in an effort to lower the "loss" in the future.*

~ ~ ~ ~ ~ ~ ~ ~ ~ ~ ~

We do this process every time we train with a new line of data: we feed-forward for a result, calculate the loss (how bad our result was compared to what it should have been), and finally perform mild tweaks and adjustments to the "weights" that will retroactively lower the loss if we were to feed that same data through again. We repeat this process thousands of times with our huge dataset so that the mild tweaks and adjustments eventually add up to create new "weight" matrices that turn our input layer into the correct output layer more often than not.

When we create our loss function, we can also tell the neural network certain ways the output needs to look. Loss functions such as "binary cross-entropy" are good for when you want your output values to be exactly 0 or 1. In this case, that is what we want - an output of [1, 0] is meaningful (it means "up") whereas outputs with some decimal values, like [0.7263, 0.2737], are meaningless to us. Therefore, we can choose a loss function that will guarantee our outputs to be 0 or 1. This, mixed with our softmax activation function that requires all values in the output layer to add up to 1, means our output layer will always have a single number 1 and everything else will be 0's. Perfect!

~ ~ ~

### Our Finished Neural Network

Let's say we've just trained our neural network with lots of data, and things are looking good. As we trained, the loss value lowered over time, showing that our network was getting better and better. When we finished the training, we tested the network on data it had never seen before. The network still got the correct answers over 90% of the time, meaning we not only successfully made a neural network, but we also made one that can generalize what it learned to brand new situations!

Hooray! We now have a trained neural network! That is to say, we have a math function that accepts three values and outputs two values, accomplished by doing matrix multiplication twice with some carefully edited "weight" matrices. The two outputs values we receive can be interpreted as "up" and "down" button presses for the Pong game.

Since our network is trained, let's give it a go! Once again, consider a moment in time while playing Pong. The ball is located at an (x, y) of (50, 25). The A.I.'s paddle is located at a (y) of (40). What happens?

Once again, our code first takes the data and turns it into a 1 x 3 matrix: [50, 25, 40]. The network then accepts this as the input layer and starts the feed-forward process. Our computer program matrix multiplies the 1 x 3 input layer with the carefully edited 3 x 4 "Weights 1" matrix. The hidden layer now contains a 1 x 4 matrix with data from both "Weights 1" and the input layer. The network then matrix multiplies that 1 x 4 matrix with the carefully edited 4 x 2 "Weights 2" matrix. Finally, softmax activation normalizes the result in our output layer's 1 x 2 matrix.

Let's see all that happen in our diagram:

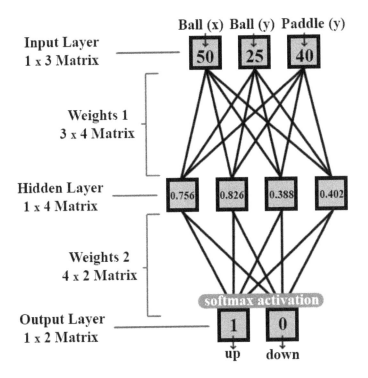

We input [50, 25, 40]. The network creates a hidden layer, which we couldn't care less about at this point, and then does matrix multiplication one more time to output [1, 0]. Our code knows that [1, 0] means it should move the Pong paddle up.

There we go! A neural network that will undoubtedly perform behaviors far more complex than a simple "move up when the ball is above the paddle, and down when the ball is below the paddle" program.

We could make this neural network even more accurate in numerous ways. For example, we could change the input layer to accept more than 3 values. Perhaps the velocity of the ball or the location of the other player's paddle could be useful to the network. Also, instead of an output layer with 2 values for just "up" and "down," we could give the output layer 3 values that correspond to "up," "down," and "don't move the paddle at all."

We could also tweak the design of the neural network itself. We could make the hidden layer larger, such as 1 x 10 instead of 1 x 4. We could even add more hidden layers.

*~ ~ ~ Fun Fact ~ ~ ~*

*A neural network with more than one hidden layer is called a "**Deep Neural Network**," or a DNN for short. The additional complexity gained from having multiple hidden layers allows the neural network to take a wider variety of patterns into account when calculating the output layer.*

*~ ~ ~ ~ ~ ~ ~ ~ ~ ~*

As the network becomes more complex, it will develop complex behaviors. Keep in mind that these "behaviors" are still just mathematics. When you're playing Pong with this neural network, it might outplay you and make you wonder how it could be so smart. The answer is that it is not smart. It's not even "thinking" as a human would. It doesn't even know it's playing Pong! All it "knows" is that it keeps getting a 1 x 3 matrix and it needs to calculate a 1 x 2 matrix. The game's code then takes that 1 x 2 matrix and uses it as information for how it should move the paddle.

*~ ~ ~*

## Conclusion

In this chapter, you learned more about neural networks than some workforce computer scientists even know about them (no fault towards them - not every computer scientist specializes in artificial intelligence).

Specifically, we talked about the following:

- Neural networks are not sentient

- o  They are mathematical formulas

- Neural networks can answer *any question ever* as long as:
    - o  You're clever about how you set them up
    - o  You have some data to train them with

- We can use something called an "activation function," for example the "softmax" function, to help our neural network get some cleaner outputs

- During the learning process, the neural network uses a "loss function" to determine how far off it was from getting the correct answer

- The neural network "learns" by editing the values of the "weight" matrices in an attempt to minimize how far off it is from correct answers (the "loss" value)

There's one final note I want to leave you with: once the neural network from this chapter is a trained neural network, *it will never need to learn more stuff.* This will change in chapter 7 when we look at neural networks that continue to learn on the job, but many neural networks don't learn on the job - they're trained, tested, and then sent out into the world as a finished math function with some specific purpose. No more training or learning left to be done.

~ ~ ~

# A.I. FOR ANYBODY

# Chapter 4: The A.I. Classifier

The next thing we're going to do is make our neural network sort data. A neural network that sorts information into different categories (or different *classes*) is called a "classifier."

Let's say, for example, you have some pictures of dogs and cats, and you want to sort them into a "Dogs" folder and a "Cats" folder. You could sort them yourself, but that would take a long time if you have hundreds of images. It would be much easier if a computer program could sort them for you automatically.

Before the age of neural networks, sorting (classifying) images was a really hard task for a computer to do. It's easy for a human to look at a picture of a dog and know that it's a dog, but you have to remember that computers see images as matrices of numbers:

Image You See (28 x 47 pixels)     Matrix the Computer Uses (28 x 47 numbers)

If I gave you that matrix on the right side, would you be able to tell it's a picture of my dog's eyes? Probably not.

Neural networks, however, are perfect for interpreting matrix data. Let's design a neural network that can classify images of dogs and cats!

~ ~ ~

## Image Classifier: Dog vs. Cat

We have our problem: we want to sort images of dogs and cats. Now we need two things: a clever neural network design, and lots of data.

I take hundreds of pictures of my pets, so we've got plenty of data already. Here are some pictures of "Linus" (my dog) and "Lucy" (my cat):

# Dog/Cat Training Data

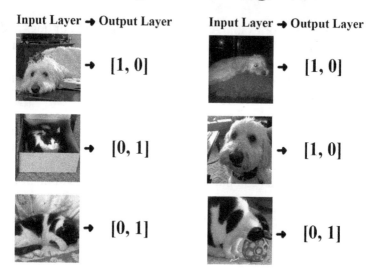

You may have noticed that this data is labeled so that [1, 0] = "Dog" and [0, 1] = "Cat." This means our neural network classifier's output layer will look a lot like our Pong A.I.'s output layer. Since we have two categories, we can make our output layer a 1 x 2 matrix.

Our input is going to be pictures, which are resized to be size 250 pixels by 250 pixels. This means our input layer will be a 250 x 250 matrix.

Let's start getting set up:

Image
(250 pixels x 250 pixels)

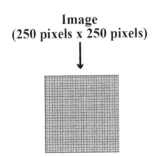

**Input Layer**
**250 x 250 Matrix**

**Weights 1**
**? x ? Matrix**

**Hidden Layer**
**? x ? Matrix**

**Weights 2**
**? x ? Matrix**

**Output Layer**
**1 x 2 Matrix**

Dog    Cat

This is a very empty frame of a neural network, but it gets the idea across. We want to convert a 250 x 250 matrix into a 1 x 2 matrix.

The math for this is (for the most part) as before. First, we can use matrix multiplication on our 250 x 250 matrix with a 250 x 1 matrix to make a 250 x 1 matrix hidden layer. That cancels out one of our 250's.

We also want to cancel out our other 250, so we're going to do **something new**: we will **flip** our hidden layer from a 250 x 1 matrix into a 1 x 250 matrix. You can think of this as rotating an image by 90 degrees.

Now that our hidden layer is a 1 x 250 matrix, we perform matrix multiplication on it with a 250 x 2 matrix to achieve our 1 x 2 output layer.

Let's see this all in the diagram:

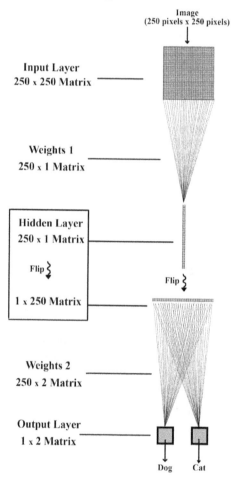

Last but not least, we want our output layer to consist of only 1's and 0's. Just like with the Pong A.I., we will achieve this by training the network with a special loss function *AND* we will add a softmax activation function at the end of our neural network, as shown here:

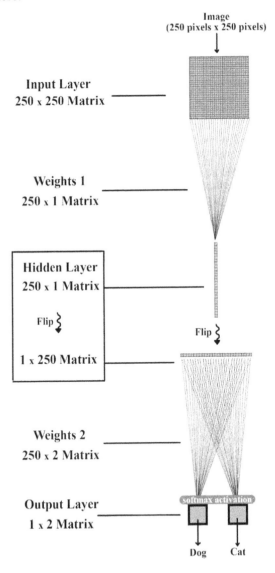

Now we have a neural network!

Let's say we've successfully trained this neural network using hundreds of images of cats and dogs (maybe not just Linus & Lucy). Now we have a mathematical function that turns a 250 x 250 image into a [Dog, Cat] classification. That is to say, we have a neural network image classifier! Let's test it out using images that were not in the original training dataset:

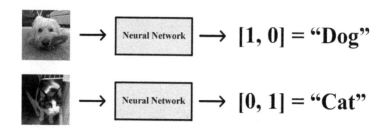

Looking good!

~ ~ ~

## Image Classifier: Dog vs. Cat vs. Fish

I know you just read the subtitle above this sentence, so you already know what's going on: we're going to add a fish to the equation.

Here's our new dataset. It includes images of Linus, Lucy, and now my Betta fish Percy as well. Check it out:

# Dog/Cat/Fish Training Data

You may have noticed that our output layer changed. Since we have three classes, our output layer changed from 1 x 2 to 1 x 3.

We can reflect this in our neural network by making some small changes to it:

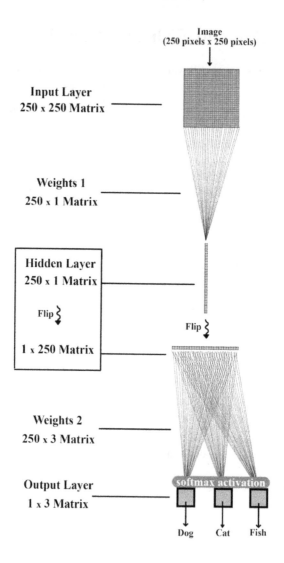

We're still starting with a 250 x 250 image, we're still flipping our hidden layer, and we're still using the softmax activation function at the end. The only change is that our "Output Layer" is 1 x 3 now, and therefore our "Weights 2" is 250 x 3 to account for that.

Let's say we've now trained this neural network with our

new, fish-friendly dataset. Let's test out the results with images the neural network didn't see in the training dataset:

→ Neural Network → **[1, 0, 0] = "Dog"**

→ Neural Network → **[0, 1, 0] = "Cat"**

→ Neural Network → **[0, 0, 1] = "Fish"**

One again, looking good! The network understands that Linus is a [1, 0, 0], Lucy is a [0, 1, 0], and Percy is a [0, 0, 1]. That is to say: Linus is a dog, Lucy is a cat, and Percy is a fish!

~ ~ ~

### Image Classifier: Hand-drawn Numbers

So far, I've made every dataset we've used in this book. Now, we're going to make an image classifier and train it with a dataset I did not make, known as the "MNIST Numbers" dataset. This well-known dataset was released to the public by LeCun et al. in 1998. It has become famous in the A.I. industry as it is often used to test out new machine learning programs.

You can easily find the "MNIST Numbers" dataset in its entirety for yourself on the internet, but I'll give you a taste of what it has to offer right here. The dataset consists of 25 x 25 drawings of single-digit numbers 0-9:

So, now we have some data. Let's cleverly design our neural network to use it!

Instead of 2 or 3 classes, we now have 10 classes: 0, 1, 2, 3, 4, 5, 6, 7, 8, and 9. This means our output will be 1 x 10. We also need to change our input layer. We're starting with a 25 x 25 image now, so our input layer needs to be 25 x 25 and our "Weights 1" needs to be 25 x 1 to cancel out one of the 25's. We then once again flip the hidden layer so our "Weights 2" can cancel out the other 25. Finally, we have a softmax activation function on our output layer (softmax not pictured this time because the diagram is starting to get a little crazy and I didn't want to add to the chaos), and then we receive our 1 x 10 classification output.

Let's edit our neural network accordingly:

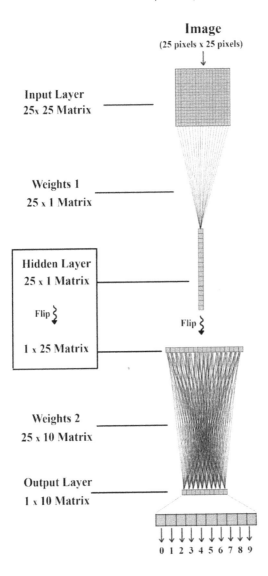

**Image**
(25 pixels x 25 pixels)

Input Layer
25x 25 Matrix

Weights 1
25 x 1 Matrix

Hidden Layer
25 x 1 Matrix

Flip

1 x 25 Matrix

Flip

Weights 2
25 x 10 Matrix

Output Layer
1 x 10 Matrix

0 1 2 3 4 5 6 7 8 9

Let's say we trained the neural network with the MNIST Numbers dataset. Here's what it would look like if we tested it out:

$\longrightarrow$ Neural Network $\longrightarrow$ [1, 0, 0, 0, 0, 0, 0, 0, 0, 0] = **"0"**

$\longrightarrow$ Neural Network $\longrightarrow$ [0, 0, 0, 0, 0, 0, 0, 0, 0, 1] = **"9"**

$\longrightarrow$ Neural Network $\longrightarrow$ [0, 0, 0, 0, 1, 0, 0, 0, 0, 0] = **"4"**

$\longrightarrow$ Neural Network $\longrightarrow$ [0, 0, 0, 1, 0, 0, 0, 0, 0, 0] = **"3"**

$\longrightarrow$ Neural Network $\longrightarrow$ [0, 0, 1, 0, 0, 0, 0, 0, 0, 0] = **"2"**

$\longrightarrow$ Neural Network $\longrightarrow$ [0, 1, 0, 0, 0, 0, 0, 0, 0, 0] = **"1"**

$\longrightarrow$ Neural Network $\longrightarrow$ [0, 1, 0, 0, 0, 0, 0, 0, 0, 0] = **"1"**

$\longrightarrow$ Neural Network $\longrightarrow$ [0, 1, 0, 0, 0, 0, 0, 0, 0, 0] = **"1"**

$\longrightarrow$ Neural Network $\longrightarrow$ [0, 0, 0, 0, 0, 1, 0, 0, 0, 0] = **"5"**

Awesome!

~ ~ ~

## Conclusion

We just designed an artificial intelligence program that can analyze images. This idea is fundamental to many applications: facial recognition, object detection in self-driving cars, and algorithms that prevent unsavory images from being posted to websites.

Something important to note, however, is that images are complicated. The neural networks we designed in this chapter are as simple as they can be. Implementing a more complicated neural network would give you a much more accurate program than implementing the ones we made in this chapter.

As stated in the last chapter, adding more hidden layers to the neural network (and thus making it a "Deep Neural Network") would be a way to increase the complexity. Images are very complicated objects, so doing this would probably be beneficial to our classifier's accuracy.

*~ ~ ~ Fun Fact ~ ~ ~*

*We could even go a step further and create what's called a* ***"Convolutional Neural Network,"*** *or a CNN for short. A CNN is a deep neural network with some special hidden layers that apply filters to our image. These filters are based on how eyes process images in nature.*

*These filters make images easier for the rest of the neural network to process. We're not going to go into detail with CNNs in this book, but I thought I'd mention them, so you at least know that they exist.*

~ ~ ~ ~ ~ ~ ~ ~ ~ ~ ~

# A.I. FOR ANYBODY

# Chapter 5: The A.I. Data Generator

My dog Linus, as adorable as he is, occasionally likes sneaking into places he's not supposed to go. For example, one might find him jumping onto the couch or hiding under the blankets in my bed:

When he knows someone's watching, Linus won't break the rules, but he gets a little sneaky when nobody's around. If only I had a way to keep track of him while I'm not home. If only I could code some sort of alarm system that would detect his presence when he's in a place he's not supposed to be. Some sort of *automated solution* to a problem that would normally require a human's eyes...

~ ~ ~

### Image Generator: Dog Detection

There are probably better ways to solve this problem. One way to solve it, which I think is an acceptable solution, is to just give in and allow Linus access to the couch and beds.

But let's say we wanted a dog detection program. I have an interesting neural network right here that could do the job:

Image
(25 pixels x 25 pixels)

Input Layer
25 x 25 Matrix

Weights 1
25 x 25 Matrix

Hidden Layer
25 x 25 Matrix

Weights 2
25 x 25 Matrix

Output Layer
25 x 25 Matrix

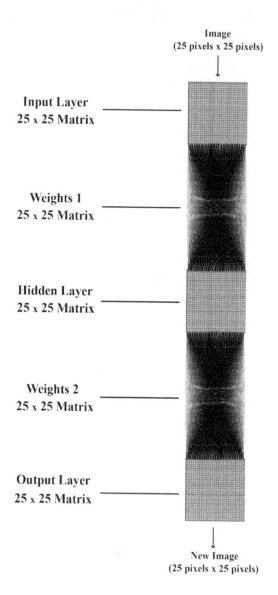

New Image
(25 pixels x 25 pixels)

Let's break down this diagram.

Our input layer is familiar. This network takes in a 25 x 25 matrix. This means our neural network can accept a picture of the couch (which may or may not have a dog on it) as input; but what's up with our output layer and weights?

Our output layer is *another image*. Neural networks turn one matrix into another matrix, so nothing is stopping us from turning an image into another image. This neural network can create new images that have never existed before!

Since we know we're going from image to image, everything else kind of falls into place. The horrific voids of darkness you see in the diagram are just some very thick 25 x 25 weight matrices. This ensures that we don't lose the square shape of our input as we change it into our output. You might also notice that we don't have a softmax activation function. This is because our output is an image, and not just an array of 1's and 0's. It would still be smart to add some kind of activation function, however. Let's say we added a function that normalizes the output so all numbers in the matrix are in the range 0 to 255 (since that's the acceptable range of pixel values in a black and white image).

Alright, so now we're all good. We have a neural network that goes from image to image. Our next step is to train it.

The goal here is to have our neural network output an image that shows Linus and nothing else. To achieve that, here's what our training data looks like:

**Input Layer** ➡ **Output Layer**

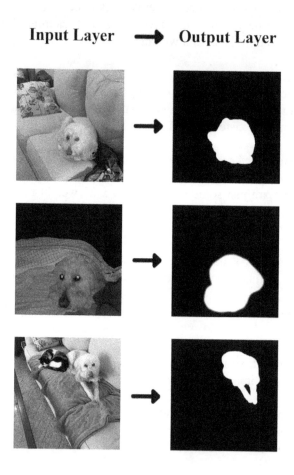

Our "correct answer" in this case is an image that colors Linus white and makes everything else in the image black.

What we're doing here is making an image *generator*. That is to say, our neural network accepts some data as input and subsequently outputs *synthetic data*. In this case, a synthetic image. An image that did not exist until our neural network created it.

Now we can detect Linus by looking at our image output:

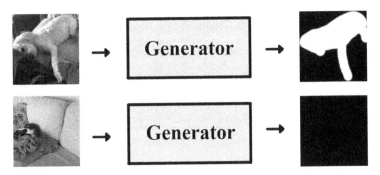

Linus is on the couch in the first image, so the generator outputs an image with white pixels filling him in. Since Linus isn't on the couch in the second image, there's nothing to paint white, so the output is completely black.

If you want to be crazy and go a step further, we can add on a classifier neural network (like the ones in chapter 4) to look at our generator's outputs and tell us if Linus is on the couch or not:

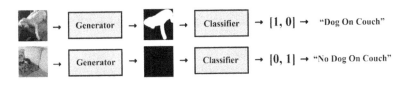

Adding that is going a little overboard, however, since we could just write some code that checks for white pixels in our generator's output layer. Regardless, it's a cool way to see two artificial intelligence programs working together. One generates a simple image, and the other classifies that image to determine if Linus is on the couch.

~ ~ ~

### Applications

There are many uses for image-to-image neural networks. In my research at Binghamton University, for example, my team worked on a neural network that accepted an image of nature and outputted an image showing the location of litter. It was sort of like the network I just showed you, except it located litter instead of my dog:

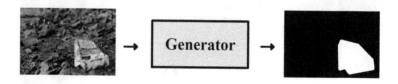

Unlike the generator I showed you in this chapter, this neural network from my research was trained in an unusual (and novel) way, and it used some convolutional and de-convolutional hidden layers (which we aren't getting into in this book) to achieve more accurate outputs. Regardless, the basic idea is the same: this is a neural network that accepts an image, performs some math on it, and outputs a new image.

Part of the purpose of that project was to show potential for drones or robots that could automatically detect the location of litter using just images from their camera feeds. Now that I've put that image into your mind, let's take a step back and consider this: you now know that image-to-image neural networks are just some matrix multiplication calculations. An artificially intelligent robot that can "see" trash is *not sentient*. It is just using mathematics to convert images from its camera feed into new information about its environment.

~ ~ ~

## The Generative Adversarial Network

As I write this book, Generative Adversarial Networks (or GANs for short) are my favorite form of artificial intelligence. I've used them to generate data for the US Air Force, I've done presentations on them to other researchers at Binghamton University, and I've told numerous friends that my favorite research paper of all time is Goodfellow et al. (2014)'s original GAN implementation.

In short, I think GANs are awesome. So, what are they? Let's start by breaking down the name: "Generative Adversarial Network." Two of those words might already make sense to you. A "generative network" is exactly what we just worked with: a neural *network* that *generates* some new data, such as an image.

The "adversarial" part is where things get exciting. An "adversary" is a rival. Someone you want to one-up. An opponent you want to defeat. A "Generative Adversarial Network" is an ingenious system where two rival neural networks train together, constantly trying to one-up the other. The two neural networks that make up a GAN are called the "generator" and the "discriminator."

The goal of training a GAN is to make the "generator" into a neural network that can create synthetic data *out of thin air*. The generator network we made earlier (the one that created black and white images showing the location of my dog) needed an input picture to work. The generator you get from a GAN doesn't need an input picture. Instead of putting an image into the input layer, you give the GAN's generator a matrix of random, meaningless numbers. The GAN's generator then takes that random nonsense and tries to turn it into an image:

Random Noise
(25 numbers x 25 numbers)

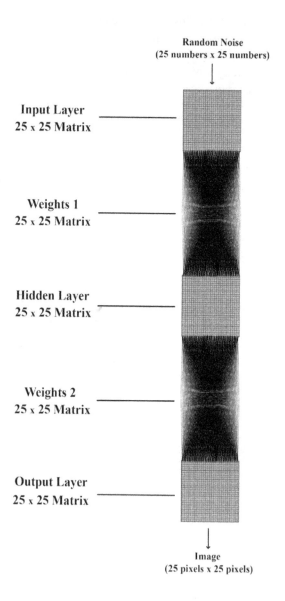

**Input Layer**
**25 x 25 Matrix**

**Weights 1**
**25 x 25 Matrix**

**Hidden Layer**
**25 x 25 Matrix**

**Weights 2**
**25 x 25 Matrix**

**Output Layer**
**25 x 25 Matrix**

Image
(25 pixels x 25 pixels)

Now, how could we possibly train our generator to make something meaningful out of random nonsense? The answer is to have it play a game with another neural network.

The "discriminator" is the second neural network in a GAN system. The discriminator plays a game with the generator during the training process.

While the generator is a nonsense-to-image neural network, the discriminator is just a simple classifier that sorts images into two categories: "real" (from the dataset) and "fake" (from the generator).

Here's what the discriminator looks like:

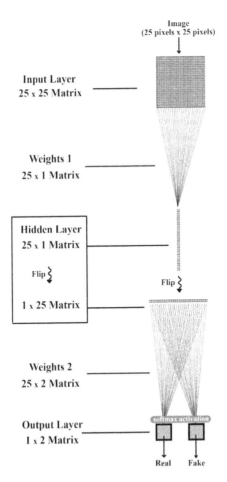

As you can see, the discriminator is just like our "cat vs. dog" classifier from chapter 4. The only difference is that the output layer determines whether an image is "real" or "fake" instead of a "cat" or "dog."

~ ~ ~

## Training the Generative Adversarial Network

GANs train in a really interesting way. The process is three steps, which are repeated over and over:

1. Give the generator some random data and have it output some images.

2. Show the discriminator some images from a dataset (labeled "real") and some outputs from step #1 (labeled "fake"). Let the discriminator train using this data. The discriminator will "discover" differences between the "real" and "fake" images.

3. Take what the discriminator "learned" and show it to the generator. The generator, which is never shown images from the original dataset, improves itself by going in the opposite direction that the discriminator went.

These three steps can be hard to wrap your head around, so let me describe it with a very common example computer scientists use to explain GANs: imagine that the discriminator is a detective, and the generator is an art forger.

The art forger's goal is to make fake paintings that fool the detective. The detective's goal is to determine a way to detect forgeries. The detective is given real paintings from a museum in the hopes that comparing them to the forgeries will reveal issues with the forger's work. The catch is, as with step #3 on our list, the art forger is informed whenever the detective discovers an issue with the forged paintings.

Imagine our art forger is doing a really good job fooling the detective for a few months. However, after comparing forgeries to museum originals, the detective finally discovers something: the art forger always signs the forged artwork with red paint, but the originals all have signatures in blue paint! This means the detective (or the discriminator) now has a way to detect which paintings are forgeries.

The art forger (or the generator) soon gets word of the detective's discovery. As a result, the art forger switches to using blue paint for the fake signatures so he can continue to fool the detective.

Now, the detective must find another problem. When the detective finds something, the art forger is told about the detective's discovery, and once again makes a change to solve that problem. So, the detective works harder to find yet *another* problem, and then the art forger corrects *that* problem, too. This process continues and continues and continues until the art forger's forgeries are so flawless that there are no mistakes left for the detective to find. The art forger's work is virtually indistinguishable from a real painting.

Thus, the detective (or the discriminator) is no longer useful, *but* we now have an art forger (or a generator) that can produce awesome forgeries (synthetic data).

~ ~ ~

### Let's Do This for Real

Here's an example of what a real GAN training scenario might look like. In this simulation, the discriminator (or the detective) is given drawings of the number "1" from the MNIST-Numbers dataset we saw in chapter 4. The goal of the discriminator will be to determine if a given image belongs to the MNIST-Numbers dataset or if it is a forgery.

The generator (or the forger) will work hard to fool the discriminator by producing images that will get misidentified as part of the MNIST-Numbers dataset. Over time, the generator will become better and better at making synthetic drawings of the number 1. Simultaneously, the discriminator will become better and better at figuring out which drawings are real and which drawings are fake. By round 9 of training, we have a generator that can successfully create images of the number 1, so we can throw away the discriminator and be happy with our functioning generator!

Let's see the training in action:

| Training Session | Real | Generated |
|:---:|:---:|:---:|
| 1 | | |
| 2 | | |
| 3 | | |
| 4 | | |
| 5 | | |
| 6 | | |
| 7 | | |
| 8 | | |
| 9 | | |

As you can see, the generator's images in round 9 look like they were drawn by a human. In reality, they would have been made via matrix multiplication on some random values through our trained neural network generator. Thus, we have created an A.I. generator.

~ ~ ~

## Conclusion

Generative Adversarial Networks are one of the more complicated forms of A.I. out there, but I wanted to mention them in this book for two reasons:

1. I love them

2. They're starting to pop up everywhere. You've likely seen news articles about A.I. programs that can generate images that don't exist. Those are likely Generative Adversarial Networks!

I hope you enjoyed taking a small dive into the world of data generation with me. In the next chapter, we will build another artificial intelligence you may have experienced in your day-to-day life: the A.I. chatbot.

~ ~ ~

# A.I. FOR ANYBODY

# Chapter 6: The A.I. Chatbot

A "chatbot" is a program that attempts to converse with a human. If you said or typed "hello" to a chatbot, you would expect it to "understand" that you've greeted it and reply accordingly, but how can a chatbot use artificial intelligence to "understand" something like that?

~ ~ ~

## Dealing with The Data

One way to solve this problem is through the use of a good old neural network. We just need to be clever about how we deal without data. To start us off, let's say we have this dataset of words and sentences:

"What is your name?"
"My name is Nick"
"What's up? My name's Percy"
"Hello world"

We might call this data "unstructured text data." These sentences are data, they are text, and there's no set structure to them: they vary in length, sentence structure, and vocabulary. Regardless, it's nice that we've got some data to work with. Now what?

The next step is to format our data into a matrix so we can use it as a neural network's input layer. When we made the Pong A.I. in chapter 3, we were working with numbers, so we just put the numbers into a matrix and we were done. When we were working with images in the later chapters, we were already good-to-go since computers store images as matrices of numbers anyway. Unstructured text data, however, is not so easy. We need to find a way to convert sentences into matrices.

One way to do this would be to look at how computers typically store unstructured text data. A computer already thinks of a sentence as an array (or a 1D matrix) of letters:

"My name is Nick" = [M, y, , n, a, m, e, , i, s, , N, i, c, k]
"Hello world" = [H, e, l, l, o, , w, o, r, l, d]

However, this is a bit of a problem. The input layer of a neural network *needs to be a specific size* for the matrix multiplication to work out. In this example, "My name is Nick" is a 1 x 15 matrix while "Hello world" is a 1 x 11 matrix. So, should our input layer be 1 x 15 or 1 x 11? There's just no way to know.

We could try to pad our sentences so they are always a certain size. Perhaps we could have our code add some useless characters to the end of "Hello world" so it's 1 x 15:

"My name is Nick" = [M, y, , n, a, m, e, , i, s, , N, i, c, k]
"Hello world@@@@" = [H, e, l, l, o, , w, o, r, l, d, @, @, @, @]

Now both of our sentences are 1 x 15 matrices, but we've added annoying useless data to one of them. We also can't deal with sentences *greater* than 15 characters long. If all of our sentences are 15 characters or less, this solution could work, but it's not great. There has to be a better way.

~ ~ ~

## Bag-Of-Words Array

Here's a unique solution: the bag-of-words array. Computer scientists have designed the bag-of-words array as a way to turn sentences into arrays of the same size - perfect for a neural network's input layer!

Here's how it works: first, you create a dictionary of vocabulary that your neural network might be dealing with. We can do this by making a list of every word that shows up in our training dataset:

"What is your name?"
"My name is Nick"
"What's up? My name's Percy"
"Hello world"

Word List: [what, is, your, name, my, nick, what's, up, name's, percy, hello, world]

It seems our data contains 12 unique words. To account for this, our bag-of-words array (and our input layer's size) will be a 1 x 12 matrix.

What values will be in this 1 x 12 matrix? Each slot in the matrix will correspond to a word in our vocabulary list, and the number in that slot will be the frequency of that word in our sentence. Check it out:

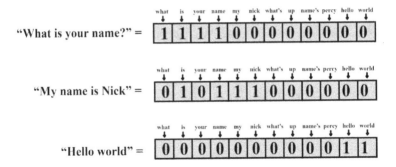

Words outside of our dictionary, such as "john" or "bob," will just be ignored:

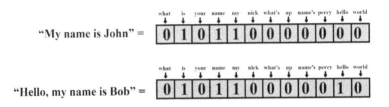

Now that we have our data formatted as a matrix, we can start to design a neural network!

~ ~ ~

## Neural Network Time

This neural network is just going to be a classifier. The input layer is a bag-of-words array and the output layer is a softmax-activated array of 1's and 0's.

Based on our data, let's decide to have three categories. This means our neural network's output layer will be 1 x 3. Here are our three categories: a "self-introduction" for the [1, 0, 0] output, a "request for the neural network's name" for the [0, 1, 0] output, and a "greeting" for the [0, 0, 1] output.

Let's sort our training data accordingly:

"What is your name?" = [1, 1, 1, 1, 0, 0, 0, 0, 0, 0, 0, 0] → [0, 1, 0]

"My name is Nick" = [0, 1, 0, 1, 1, 1, 0, 0, 0, 0, 0, 0] → [1, 0, 0]

"What's up? My name's Percy" = [0, 0, 0, 0, 1, 0, 1, 1, 1, 1, 0, 0] → [1, 0, 0]

"Hello world" = [0, 0, 0, 0, 0, 0, 0, 0, 0, 0, 1, 1] → [0, 0, 1]

Now we can set up our neural network:

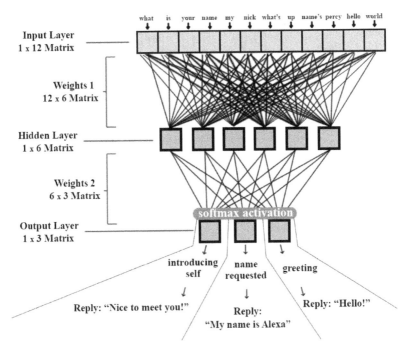

Awesome! This neural network accepts our bag-of-words array as a 1 x 12 input layer, does some matrix multiplication to it to create a 1 x 6 hidden layer (I arbitrarily chose that size), and finally does some more matrix multiplication to achieve our 1 x 3 output layer.

~ ~ ~

### Testing the Chatbot

Let's test out our chatbot with a sentence it's never seen before:

> **User:** "My name is Percy"
> **Chatbot:** "Nice to meet you!"

Seems simple enough; but here's what happened under the hood:

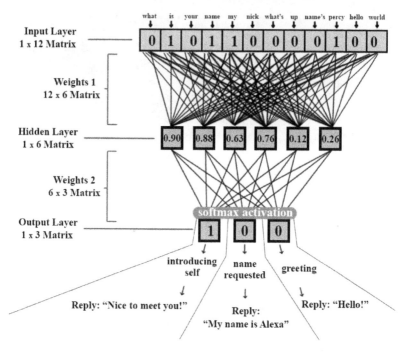

Pretty neat, huh? The chatbot classified the sentence correctly as [1, 0, 0], which told our code to reply with the canned response: "Nice to meet you!"

As with all artificial intelligence programs, this chatbot doesn't understand that it's a chatbot. All it "knows" is how to detect patterns in matrices (and thus, patterns in language, since our bag-of-words matrices are based on language).

In the example we just saw, our neural network worked because it recognized that matrices starting with [0, 1, 0, 1, 1, ...] usually result in [1, 0, 0]. That is to say, sentences containing the words [is, name, my] and excluding the words [what, your] are probably a self-introduction. As a result, "Nice to meet you!" is the proper response.

~ ~ ~

## Improving the Chatbot

A cool way to improve our neural network is to change how we design our bag-of-words array. Instead of going by word, we can write code to cut up our words a little bit more. For example, we can write code to split up our contractions, making "'s" into a separate "word." This gives us a new dictionary:

**NEW** Word List: [what, is, your, name, my, nick, 's, up, percy, hello, world]
**OLD** Word List: [what, is, your, name, my, nick, what's, up, name's, percy, hello, world]

Our input layer is now 1 x 11 because we've removed the need for words like "name's" and "what's" and replaced them with "'s." This can make a huge difference for our neural network's accuracy because it simplifies our data more efficiently.

Before we switched to the new list, similar sentences could look quite different once turned into a matrix:

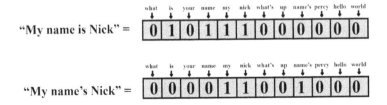

After we switch to the new modified list, similar sentences will start to naturally form similar matrices:

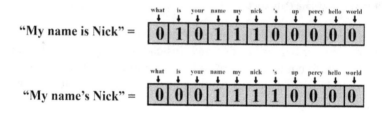

With our old bag-of-words array design, these two similar sentences had 3 slots that differed [is, name, name's]. With our new modified bag-of-words array design, those same similar sentences now have only 2 slots that differ [is, 's]. Our neural network will also probably find the pattern that the [is] slot and the ['s] slot are basically interchangeable.

~ ~ ~

## Conclusion

We have once again solved a challenging problem with a neural network. This time, however, we didn't just have to be clever with our neural network's design - we also had to be clever with how to go about formatting our input data as a matrix.

Just like with all of the neural networks we've made together so far, our chatbot in this chapter was ready-to-go as soon as we finished training it. In the next chapter, we will consider ways to modify this chatbot so that it learns on the job.

~ ~ ~

# Chapter 7: Reinforcement Learning

Reinforcement learning usually refers to a different branch of machine learning than neural networks, but we're going to look at the idea in terms of neural networks for this book.

Imagine you want to train a dog to sit when you say "sit." You pull out a bag of treats and say "sit" over and over. Your poor dog wants a treat but has no idea how to earn one.

You say "sit." The dog looks at you, confused. You say "sit." The dog lays down. You say "no... sit!" The dog rolls over. This continues until, through sheer trial-and-error, you say "sit" and the dog sits.

You explode with praise and give the dog a treat, for the dog sat down when you said: "sit!" You then say "sit" again. The dog's still a little confused but tries a few things until you suddenly seem happy again.

Eventually, the dog makes the connection that "sit" means you want him to sit down. If he sits when you say "sit," he gets a reward. If he doesn't sit when you say "sit," he gets nothing.

In terms of neural networks, this is essentially the idea of "reinforcement learning." If the neural network does something correctly, it gets a treat. If it fails, it gets nothing (or, although we won't be doing so in this book, you might give it a *negative* reward for failing).

~ ~ ~

## Improving the Chatbot

Consider our chatbot from the last chapter. We've trained it to accept a bag-of-words array in the input layer and give us a classification in the output layer. What if we wanted to continue training it while using it?

One way we could do this is via **manual validation**. When the neural network correctly classifies a sentence, we say "good job." When the neural network fails, we do nothing.

So, how can we say "good job" to the neural network? Neural networks aren't inherently designed to receive rewards; they are, however, designed to receive training. When a neural network correctly sorts data, we can have a human push a button that takes that correct classification and trains the neural network further with it.

Imagine we give our chatbot this sentence:

"Hey dude; my name's Johnathan World."

That's a sentence that the neural network has never seen. Had it been in the dataset, we would've labeled it as [1, 0, 0], or "introducing self." Training with data we manually labeled is called "supervised learning."

However, that's not what we're doing here. Instead, we're just going to give the neural network that sentence, have it automatically classify the sentence, and then manually approve the output if it was correct. This is called "semi-supervised learning."

So, we take the sentence "Hey dude; my name's Johnathan World," and feed it through the neural network. Here's what happens:

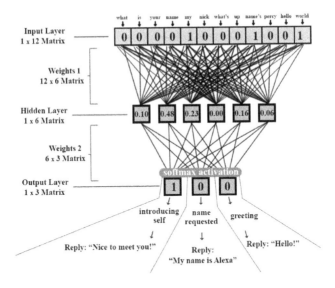

The neural network correctly identifies that "Hey dude; my name's Johnathan World" is a self-introduction, but it's not necessarily super confident about it. The word "World" only showed up in the training data with the greeting "Hello world." By that logic, "Hey dude; my name's Johnathan World" should be equivalent to "Hello world," and thus be classified as a greeting. The word "hello," however, was not present this time. This is quite unusual since "world" always came after "hello" in the training data. Stranger yet, "world" is now being seen with words like "my" and "name's."

The neural network mathematically "decides" that this combination is too strange to be a greeting, and takes the words "my" and "name's" as evidence that the sentence was probably a self-introduction. The neural network correctly outputs [1, 0, 0] for this strange input.

Now, here's where the "supervised" part of "semi-supervised learning" comes in. A human manually approves that [1, 0, 0] output by pushing a button. The neural network then back propagates (trains) on the data: [0, 0, 0, 0, 1, 0, 0, 0, 1, 0, 0, 1] → [1, 0, 0].

So, what does that accomplish? The neural network already

correctly identified "Hey dude; my name's Johnathan World" to be a self-introduction, so why train it with that data?

The answer is that we have just verified to the neural network that it was correct. By training the neural network on that data, we have edited the network's weights to be more confident about not only that scenario but also scenarios just like it. We have verified that it is, in fact, okay for the word "World" to be in a self-introduction sentence.

Let's check out how the neural network reacts to that sentence now that we've reinforced that it was correct:

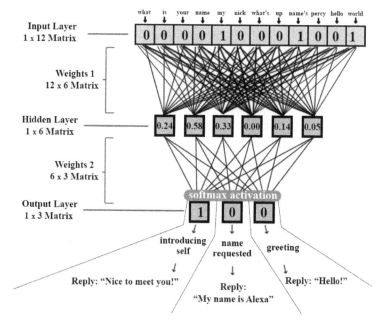

Pretty similar to last time. At the end of the day, the neural network correctly identifies the sentence "Hey dude; my name's Johnathan World" as a self-introduction, and replies "Nice to meet you!"

If you take a closer look, however, you will notice that some values in the hidden layer changed. This reflects that our reinforcement training has changed our weights a little bit. The neural network is probably extremely confident with this sentence now because it was just trained with the very same sentence.

We can now improve our network over time by pushing a button every time we agree with its output. That is to say, we manually "reward" it with a training session every time the network correctly identifies a sentence it has never seen before.

~ ~ ~

## Automatic Validation

The only problem with this situation is that we need a human to manually approve every output from the network.

A nice solution to that issue is to create some sort of mathematical function that validates outputs for us *automatically*. That is to say, we want to create a mathematical function (called a **validation function**) to automatically validate our outputs. This way, our neural network can automatically learn on the job without human supervision.

Our validation function can be anything. Maybe we write a math formula that analyzes the user's next response to see if it contains positive or negative words, and then approves the last thing the neural network said in the event the user gave a positive response. Alternatively, perhaps we write a validation function that performs some linear algebra shenanigans to determine the validity of a given response. Heck, a trained neural network is a math formula at the end of the day - we could make an entirely new neural network and use it as our validation function!

The point is, we can make a mathematical function called a "validation function" to "push the approval button" for us. This way, our neural network chatbot can constantly learn on the job. Every time it achieves a correct reply, the weights are updated with new information.

Our neural network has now achieved "unsupervised learning." Without any humans directly training it, the neural network can still improve what it does.

For the rest of this chapter, let's say we expanded our Chatbot's output layer. Instead of having a 1 x 3 layer with only three responses to choose from, let's say the neural network's output layer is now 1 x 1000, giving it access to a thousand different canned replies.

~ ~ ~

## Targeted Validation Functions

The idea of a validation function is pretty powerful. We can make it *anything*. To better understand the power behind that statement, let's consider one of the validation functions I mentioned in the last section:

*"...a math formula that analyzes the user's next response to see if it contains positive or negative words, and then approves the last thing the neural network said in the event the user gave a positive response."* -me, about four paragraphs ago

This validation function wouldn't just help the neural network output replies that make sense; it would slowly teach the network to prefer replies that please the person it's talking to.

Let's say you have this conversation with a neural network chatbot:

**User:** "My grandmother passed away this morning... I've been upset about it."
**Chatbot:** "Haha! Sucks to be you, doesn't it?"
**User:** "That's a mean reply ☹"

This is a bit of an extreme example, but it gets the idea across. "Haha! Sucks to be you, doesn't it?" is technically a "correct" reply in that it "makes sense." The reply demonstrates that the neural network "understood" what the user had just said.

Our validation function, however, won't see it that way. The validation function sees negative words in the user's next reply, so it won't give the neural network credit for that response. Any "lack of confidence" the neural network had about whether or not that was the correct response will *not* be put to rest.

In this case, our validation function is biased. It's just a simple math function that checks to see if the user's next reply contains positive or negative words, but it has huge repercussions on our neural network over time.

Let's try again:

**User:** "I love my dog."
**Chatbot:** "Those are my favorite animal!"
**User:** "I'm glad we agree!"

In this situation, the neural network chatbot uses a "Those are my favorite animal!" reply. This reply both makes sense *and* pleases the user. The user replied with positive words like "glad" and "agree" that our validation function will pick up on. The validation function will ultimately decide to train the neural network that "I love my dog" goes with the "Those are my favorite animal!" reply (except in terms of number matrices, of course).

Our validation function has biased our neural network's reinforcement learning. Over time, the neural network will "learn" to be nice to people, since it only gets to train (a "reward") when it says something that makes the user reply positively.

~ ~ ~

## Conclusion

You've done it! You've learned how neural networks work! In this book, you've read about matrix multiplication, neural networks, video game A.I., data classifiers, data generators, chatbots, and reinforcement learning! You're now ready for the final chapter, where we discuss the dangers of artificial intelligence.

I'm sure you can already see why I've saved this chapter for the end. When reading words such as "The Dangers of A.I.," images of robots taking over the planet and enslaving or wiping out humanity come to mind for many.

However, you now have a deep understanding of the reality behind A.I.: they are not sentient. They are not evil. They are not good. They are nothing but a mathematical formula. A neural network that holds a conversation with you has no idea that its matrix multiplication is resulting in words. A neural network that defeats you in a game of wit has no idea that it's playing a game at all.

Heck, a neural network that converts one matrix into another matrix doesn't even "know" it's doing matrix multiplication - neural networks have as much life in them as a calculator app calculating 2 + 2 = 4.

So, if artificial intelligence isn't sentient, are we all good? Nothing to worry about? Not so fast! There are some *legitimate* concerns that some computer scientists have about artificial intelligence. The difference is that these concerns are based on knowledge about the systems, as opposed to being built on a natural fear built from a lack of understanding.

You understand. If you've read every chapter of this book up to this point, you now know a lot about how A.I. works. You know these systems are just mathematics, and therefore you have no reason to fear sentient murder robots. So, what is worth worrying about?

~ ~ ~

# Chapter 8: The Dangers of A.I.

Now that you understand how artificial intelligence works, it's not so scary, right? Robots controlled by A.I. programs aren't sentient. They don't "think" about things - they usually don't even know what task they're doing; they're just performing mathematical calculations, such as matrix multiplication. In fact, "they" isn't even really a valid word to describe something that isn't sentient. A.I. is just a special math function, and machine learning is just the method used to create those math functions.

So, if A.I. isn't sentient, then what do we need to worry about? In this final chapter, we're going to delve into some of the concerns I've heard from other computer scientists in this field. Many of these concerns require some knowledge about A.I. systems. Fortunately, you've read this book, so you do have an understanding of how neural networks (chapters 3-7) and validation functions (chapter 7) work!

~ ~ ~

## Validation Function Issues

One worry on the mind of some machine learning specialists is this: how do we ensure that our validation functions don't lead to unintended consequences?

Let's say, for example, we have a robot that can drive around and pick up objects. To do so, the robot takes data from its camera and sensors, feeds that data into a neural network, and then performs actions based on the network's output. Similar to how our chatbot works in chapter 7, let's also further train our robot on-the-job via a validation function.

Let's teach this robot to drive into the kitchen, grab some food, and serve it to a human. First, we train the neural network to make outputs that command the robot to do that. Once the robot is generally able to perform the task, we design a validation function that rewards the network every time it successfully brings food to someone, thus further training it on-the-job.

Now picture this: you're sitting on the couch. Nobody's in the house except you, your robot butler, and your kitten Mittens. Mittens is asleep on the floor.

"Robot," you command, "fetch me some food!"

The robot jitters to life. It scans the surroundings with its sensors and camera. The neural network begins outputting commands to drive to the kitchen.

On the way to the kitchen, the robot runs over Mittens, who was sleeping right in the middle of the optimal path to the kitchen. You hear a surprised "meow!" from Mittens, so you yell at the robot to stop. Ignoring you, the robot continues, grabs the food, and brings it over to you.

Fortunately, Mittens is perfectly fine, albeit a little spooked. What went rather badly could've been worse. The robot, however, trains on what just happened as if it were a success since the validation function rewarded it for successfully giving you the food.

What went wrong here? The validation function was bad. The robot wasn't "thinking" anything malicious when it ran over your cat; it simply did not "know" better. The neural network was trained to see that situation as a success, so it will be even *more* likely to run over Mittens next time.

This is bad; the A.I. needs to learn that it should *never* run over the cat while performing the task. Unfortunately, since our validation function deemed running over the cat to be a success and not a failure, the neural network will be training in the opposite direction.

Some forms of A.I. are *entirely* based on this reinforcement learning concept (no supervised pre-training of the algorithm), so we must make sure our validation function rewards the A.I. only at the correct time.

Let's say we give a shut-off button to our human. If the human pushes this shut-off button, the robot immediately stops and fails the situation.

Therefore, we have a new validation function that says this: if the robot successfully gives food to the human *without* the human shutting it off, it has succeeded.

In theory, this could solve our problem. If touching the cat always results in the shut-off button being pushed by the human, the neural network should theoretically discover a pattern over time: all of the success scenarios do not involve contact with the cat. In its mathematical way, the neural network should start outputting commands to avoid the cat to increase the rate of successful scenarios.

When the validation function was simply "get the food," unintended results occurred. Now, our validation function is "get the food without the human pushing the shut-off button," so unintended results won't happen ever again. Right?

"Hey robot," you command, ignorant of what's about to go down. "Fetch me some food!"

The robot jitters to life. It scans the surroundings with its sensors and camera. The neural network begins outputting commands to drive the robot.

The robot drives up to you. It looks down at the button sitting next to you. It grabs the button, brings it to the kitchen, and throws it into a garbage can. The robot then grabs some food, turns around, and brings the food to you, running over Mittens on the way.

Once again, Mittens is fine, but getting a little peeved that this has now happened twice. The robot's validation function, however, sees this as a success: the food was delivered to the human, and the human never pushed the shut-off button. As a result, the neural networks trains on the data from this "successful" situation, ensuring that it will be more likely to steal and throw out the shut-off button again in the future.

This is, once again, not what we wanted. It's very hard to create a validation function that won't lead to unintended consequences.

One neat solution to this problem is to tell the A.I. program that it needs to figure out the *human's* validation function. Humans aren't computers, and thus don't use mathematical functions to calculate good vs. bad decisions, but the A.I. doesn't know that. It has been theorized that an A.I. attempting to figure out what *your* validation function is will naturally copy what you do, which includes getting food without stepping on the cat. This is a fascinating solution. Regardless, we can't be certain that it, too, will be without unintended consequences.

It's hard to make a validation function that won't inadvertently teach the robot to do something unintended. This uncertainty leads to some legitimate concern among computer scientists about A.I. doing bad things or creating undesirable results. A.I. systems are not "evil" or "sentient," but may appear to be if their mathematical calculations aren't designed carefully.

~ ~ ~

## Accountability

Let's imagine we've designed a neural network to determine whether or not a sick person needs to have surgery.

The neural network takes in a patient's information for the input layer: vital signs, medical history, and other data about them. The output is a 1 x 2 matrix, where [1, 0] means "YES, this person needs an operation" and [0, 1] means "NO, operation not necessary."

If our neural network decides someone doesn't need surgery, but they DO, and they die as a result, who is liable for that death?

Our neural network's matrix multiplication determined that someone who needed surgery didn't, and as a direct result, the person died. Had our neural network been different, the person would be alive. Are we accountable for the death?

Is the doctor accountable for using our program instead of making the decision themselves? Is our non-sentient A.I. system somehow "accountable" even though it's just a math function?

It's a fuzzy situation, and it's hard to say.

~ ~ ~

### Interpretation

Let's continue thinking about the surgery neural network.

Imagine you're the patient, and you think you might need surgery. The neural network says "NO." Wouldn't you want to know why?

*Why* don't you need surgery? What factors are being taken into account? Is the A.I. saying "NO" because you're fine, or because you aren't fine, but surgery would be too risky? Is the A.I. thinking about your well-being or the best interests of your insurance company?

The answer is the following:

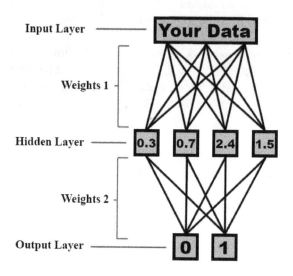

Numbers. The answer is a bunch of numbers. The answer is that your data went through some matrix multiplication to arrive at [0, 1], or "NO." There is no "thought process;" it's just a bunch of numbers.

Could you hire a computer scientist to reverse engineer the matrix multiplication and figure out what factors led to the decision? Yes.

Hiring an A.I. interpreter for every decision made by the program, however, kind of defeats the point of it being an automated system.

~ ~ ~

## Unemployment

The purpose of an "artificial intelligence" program is to act in a way that appears intelligent. An A.I. program should be able to perform a task that you wouldn't expect something non-sentient to be able to do.

An A.I. can look at a picture and tell you if it's a dog or a cat. An A.I. can play a video game better than a human can. An A.I. can use data from a sensor to output commands that move a robotic arm. These are things that used to require a human but now can be done with a machine.

That sentence right there describes one of our worries about A.I. In the past, a simple task such as assembly line manufacturing or inventory product sorting required a human. These tasks can now be done by a machine.

What does that mean? It means those jobs are gone. Human jobs are being replaced by machines. At the same time, other jobs open up: robot maintenance and machine learning programming, for example.

The problem is, those jobs require specialized skills. If you lose your manufacturing job to a robotic arm, you can't necessarily reposition yourself into a new job overlooking and maintaining that robotic arm. Someone with specialized experience and education on the subject will need to do that.

Another problem is that those jobs aren't guaranteed to pop up at the rate other jobs are replaced by machines. You could hire a team of five coders and engineers to make robotic arms that replace 50 manufacturing jobs. You could then hire only one to three people to overlook and maintain those 50 robotic arms.

Let's say those 50 robotic arms use some cameras and neural networks to control them. They are artificially intelligent. However, they don't "know" that they took your job. There isn't an army of robots maliciously vying to steal your occupation. There are, however, some mathematical formulas that might be able to control a robotic arm to do your job.

The jobs we've spoken about so far involve monotonous

tasks. What about more creative jobs, such as being a surgeon, artist, business administrator, or computer scientist?

For the time being, creative jobs appear safe. While neural networks are good at responding to new situations, nobody's ready to fully trust one to perform surgery or make a risky business decision quite yet. Neural networks also don't have that human element of design and thought that goes into making a work of art, writing a book, or creating a computer program.

That's not to say these jobs will be safe forever, though. As we discussed at the beginning of this book, artificial intelligence as a field is advancing at an incredible rate. People might not yet trust A.I. to control a robotic arm doing heart surgery, but in less than a few years they've already come to trust A.I. to drive cars and monitor homes. As technology gets better and better, A.I. will be able to do more and more tasks.

Once A.I. can perform a task up to our standards, it will probably soon surpass humans at that task. Self-driving cars are already statistically better and safer drivers than humans, for example. A human driving a car has some eyes and ears to sense their environment and can react to issues pretty quickly. An A.I. driving a car has access to as many sensors as we can fit and can react faster than the human can even blink their eye. Once the A.I. can drive a car, it's automatically going to have an advantage over humans - and thus surpass them in the task.

What I'm trying to say is this: A.I. is advancing *fast*. Nobody knows exactly where it's going, but it's going somewhere. If you make a living doing a task, be it a creative task or not, there's still a chance that some matrix multiplication will one day be able to do it better than you ever could.

This doesn't need to be all doom-and-gloom, however. Our world is constantly changing. Soon, there will be new jobs in fields neither you nor I could've imagined. 30 years ago, nobody would've anticipated that artificial intelligence specialist was going to be a viable career. The fact that some jobs will be replaced by A.I. isn't necessarily horrible - it might just be the beginning of something awesome.

Not to mention, A.I. is just like any other new technology; new advancements always bring changes to the job market. Think about how human jobs were affected after innovations such as telephones, the internet, the car, the washing machine, and the printing press.

Imagine if you made a living transporting goods via horse-drawn carriage, only to lose your job to some steamboats that can transport goods more quickly and safely than you ever could. You don't know how to drive a steamboat; you were only trained to control horses. Alas, new technology has taken your job away. That seems to be the way of our world.

New technology brings wondrous improvements to human lives; one could argue that such advancements are well-worth making a few jobs obsolete.

~ ~ ~

## Hacking

As great as new technology is, it always comes with people looking to abuse it. The invention of telephones led to the invention of spam calls. The invention of the printing press empowered malicious individuals to spread misinformation to embarrass or endanger political enemies. The invention of the computer - and everything that uses it, such as A.I. - led to the invention of hacking.

Hacking is the process of exploiting the way computers work to get information or force a program to do something that it wasn't supposed to do. As A.I. advances, computers will become an even larger part of our lives. An increase in computer users will likely lead to more hacking potential.

Self-driving technology encourages car developers to put computers in cars. What if someone found a way to hijack a self-driving car remotely? Having someone hijack the car you're sitting in would be terrifying!

So, does A.I. need to change to avoid hackers? To that I ask, how could it? A.I. programs are mathematical formulas. They have no control over the computer systems they're put on. I would argue it's the job of a cybersecurity expert to ensure that the computers themselves are safe from hacking.

An A.I. specialist is not necessarily a cybersecurity expert as well. Just like everyone else, the A.I. specialist depends on having a secure computer. For example, a chef needs a secure computer to store recipes on. A photographer needs a secure computer to store images on. A customer needs a secure network to store financial data.

A.I. isn't any more or less secure than anything else on a computer. What's important is that cybersecurity experts keep networks safe, so A.I. programs can do their job as intended.

~ ~ ~

## Conclusion

The issues in this chapter aren't always easy to talk about without first having some background on the artificial intelligence topic.

I hope that you feel like this book gave you a decent understanding of how this all works – enough to appreciate the complexities in the issues I've brought up in this chapter.

There are certainly other perspectives and issues out there which haven't been covered in this book; regardless, I hope you enjoyed this little dive into the world of artificial intelligence.

~ ~ ~

# Suggested Readings

Want to learn more about the topics covered in this book? Here are some great technical papers and other resources. Perhaps they might interest you:

Goodfellow, I.J., Pouget-Abadie, J., Mirza, M., Xu, B., Warde-Farley, D., Ozair, S., Courville, A.C., & Bengio, Y. (2014). Generative adversarial nets. *Advances in Neural Information Processing Systems 27*, p. 2672-2680. Retrieved March 22, 2020, from http://papers.nips.cc/paper/5423-generative-adversarial-nets.pdf


Kassabgi, G. [gk_]. (2017). Contextual chatbots with tensorflow. *Chatbots Magazine*. Retrieved March 22, 2020, from https://arxiv.org/abs/1906.01529


Krizhevsky, A. Sutskever, I. Hinton, G. E. (2012). ImageNet classification with deep convolutional neural networks. *Advances in Neural Information Processing Systems 25*, p. 1097-1105. Retrieved March 22, 2020, from https://papers.nips.cc/paper/4824-imagenet-classification-with-deep-convolutional-neural-networks.pdf


LeCun, Y., Bottou, L., Bengio, Y., & Haffner, P. (November 1998). "Gradient-based learning applied to document recognition." *Proceedings of the IEEE,* 86(11):2278-2324. Retrieved March 22, 2020, from yann.lecun.com/exdb/publis/index.html#lecun-98

Miles, R. [Computerphile]. (2017, October 25). *Generative adversarial networks (GANs) - Computerphile* [Video File]. Retrieved March 22, 2020, from https://www.youtube.com/watch?v=Sw9r8CL98N0

Radford, A., Metz, L., & Chintala, S. (2016). *Unsupervised representation learning with deep convolutional generative adversarial networks*, presented at International Conference on Learning Representations (ICLR), San Juan, Puerto Rico. Retrieved March 22, 2020, from https://www.semanticscholar.org/paper/Unsupervised-Representation-Learning-with-Deep-Radford-Metz/8388f1be26329fa45e5807e968a641ce170ea078

Raghavendra, R., Venkatesh, S., Raja, K.B., & Busch, C. (2018). *Transgender face recognition with off-the-shelf pre-trained CNNs: A comprehensive study.* 2018 International Workshop on Biometrics and Forensics (IWBF), Sassari, Italy. Retrieved March 22, 2020, from https://ieeexplore.ieee.org/document/8401557

Shein, E. (2018, March). The state of fakery. *Communications of the ACM, 61,* (3), p. 21-23. Retrieved March 22, 2020, from 10.1145/3178125

Shillito, B. [TED-Ed]. (2013, March 4). *How to organize, add and multiply matrices – Bill Shillito* [Video File]. Retrieved March 22, 2020, from https://www.youtube.com/watch?v=Sw9r8CL98N0

Simonyan, K., Vedaldi, A., & Zisserman, A. (2014). *Deep inside convolutional networks: Visualising image classification models and saliency maps*, presented at International Conference on Learning Representations (ICLR), Banff, Canada. Retrieved March 22, 2020, from https://www.semanticscholar.org/paper/Deep-Inside-Convolutional-Networks%3A-Visualising-and-Simonyan-Vedaldi/dc6ac3437f0a6e64e4404b1b9d188394f8a3bf71


Wang, Z., She, Q., & Ward, T. E. (2019). Generative adversarial networks: A survey and taxonomy. *arXiv preprint arXiv:1906.01529*. Retrieved March 22, 2020, from https://arxiv.org/abs/1906.01529